True Pure Land Buddhism

Jodoshinshu: An Introduction

Seigen Yamaoka

Pure Land Publications
Los Angeles

Third Printing, Revised Edition, 1991
Pure Land Publications, Los Angeles
Second Printing, 1989
Buddhist Churches of America
San Francisco
First Printing, 1989
Buddhist Churches of America
San Francisco

ISBN: 1-877604-04-6

Edited by
Pure Land Publications

Cover Design by
Ray Fukumoto

Table of Contents

Introduction

We experience many ups and downs in life. These experiences can bring us to the heights of fulfillment in one moment and to the depths of despair in the next. Because of constant change in our lives, we all seek that which allows us to face the reality of life peacefully.

Shakyamuni Buddha, the founder of Buddhism in India, taught how to face the reality of daily life in an ever changing world, and further, how to find meaning in that reality. Buddhism teaches how to be lifted beyond the small selfish island we make for ourselves and to locate ourselves in the dynamic flow of life where we have always belonged. It teaches that we must live in and be one with the flow of life, and experience the interrelated depths of "aloneness-is-non-aloneness", which is referred to as Enlightenment.

Buddhism began as a monastic practice. To attain Enlightenment, Buddhists had to leave home and loved ones, enter a monastery, and dedicate their lives to the Buddha-dharma. Unfortunately, that is extremely difficult for most of us.

Buddhism, does, however, offer another way. That way is the teachings of Buddha-dharma as interpreted by Shinran Shonin (1173-1263) of Japan, the founder of the Jodoshinshu (True Pure Land) school. Jodoshinshu is a teaching in which we are endowed with Enlightenment that is symbolized as the Pure Land. It is how we, who live a secular life with all its ups and downs, can attain Enlightenment without abandoning the secular world and entering a monastery. Traditionally, this way is called "Buddha-dharma-for-the-Householder."

But Jodoshinshu developed over 700 years ago. Are its teachings still meaningful in our modern society? To answer this question, we must understand the meaning and development of Jodoshinshu.

Jodoshinshu:
Its Meaning and Development

Living in a world of change means constantly confront-
ing the problems of happiness turning into sorrow, of
meaning turning into non-meaning, of success into failure,
and love to hate. Because we live in a world where everything is constantly compared—good with bad, rich with
poor, wise with stupid, beautiful with ugly, generous with
stingy,—we are caught in the crucial and relative bind of
drowning in suffering, or clinging to those few and fleeting
moments of happiness.

The teachings of Shakyamuni Buddha are often said to
consist of 84,000 ways to Enlightenment. What this means
is that 84,000 potential passions and desires which can deter
us from attainment are considered to exist, and that
Shakyamuni showed a way to Enlightenment for each of
those deterrents. But of the 84,000 ways, there are two
basic ways or streams of attaining Enlightenment: these are
through Self-Power and through Other-Power.

Self-Power, or self-effort, means that the responsibility
is on us to strive towards Enlightenment. We work to
perfect our being by following the example of Shakyamuni

Buddha. The monastic life is an example. The perspective is one of moving from ignorance towards Enlightenment.

Other-Power, or Buddha's Power, means that the emphasis is placed on the Buddha or Truth moving to enlighten us. Compassion is the key. The perspective is, "I am awakened to Truth," or "Truth awakens me."

Jodoshinshu, based on the life experience of Shinran Shonin, is for those of us caught in the relative human bonds of self-attachment and suffering in an ever changing world. It offers us dignity, humanity, and hope through *shinjin*, which is "the true and real mind" given to us by Amida Buddha, the personification of Enlightenment, which has the two components of Wisdom and Compassion.

Doctrinally, the heart of the Jodoshinshu teaching is that there are two aspects to merit-transference (compassionate guidance by Amida Buddha). One is the "phase of going," the process of going towards Enlightenment. The other is the "phase of returning," the process of returning to this world after attaining Enlightenment in order to lead others to the same Enlightenment.[1]

An example of this process is: In a societal relationship, we find relative comparisons which describe us as good or bad. Such relative comparisons are transcended in Jodoshinshu. In other words, we are viewed objectively as a combination of human good and bad. Shinran Shonin stated:

> From beginningless past to this day and this moment, the ocean of multitudinous beings has been defiled, evil, and filthy, and do not possess the pure

---

1   Shinran, *Kygoyshinsho*, Ryukoku Translation Series, (Ryukoku University, Kyoto, 1966), p. 29. Henceforth referred to as *RTS*.

mind; again, they have been deluded, flattering, and deceitful and do not possess the true mind.[2]

At the same time, we are also seen as being within the Wisdom and Compassion of Amida Buddha. When we are reflected in the perfection of Amida Buddha's Wisdom and Compassion, we cannot help but see how evil and ignorant we are, and how powerless we are to work out our own Enlightenment. We see that we are trapped in the growing bondage of ego-desire and self-attachment, and that the more we try to break those bonds, the more we find that we are entrenched within them. Rather than moving towards Enlightenment, we find ourselves moving away. And yet, as evil and ignorant as we are, we are the object of Amida Buddha's concern. When we are reflected in Amida Buddha's Wisdom and Compassion, we are able to see ourselves as we really are. That is when the realization arises that we can attain Enlightenment only through Other Power, meaning through Amida Buddha's Wisdom and Compassion, then that is what *shinjin*, the "true mind" is.

Shinjin is what fills our minds with joy and gratitude for being assured of Birth in the Pure Land where we will attain the same Enlightenment as Amida Buddha.

According to Jodoshinshu, Amida Buddha endows us with *shinjin*, which results in Birth in the Pure Land of Enlightenment precisely because we cannot attain Enlightenment through our own efforts. Upon being born there, we become one with Amida Buddha in the great compassionate work of saving those still caught in the web of ignorance and attachments.

This is the essence of Jodoshinshu. This approach differs from the approach to Enlightenment in general Buddhism,

2   Ibid, p. 104.

5

and it is this difference in approach that causes some difficulty in propagating the teaching of Jodoshinshu in the western world.

Sir Charles Eliot, rejected the claim that worship of Amida Buddha is Buddhist in origin. He did so for the following two reasons.

First, the central figure of Amida Buddha—*Amitabha/Amitayus* in Sanskrit, meaning "measureless light" and "measureless life," is unknown in early Buddhist literature. When Amida Buddha does appear in historical records, he does not have the same pre-eminent position that he acquired in later times.

Second, the doctrine of merit-transference (compassionate guidance by Amida Buddha), or being saved by the efforts of another, is repudiated in Early Buddhist literature. Eliot asserted that the Buddha shows how to save ourselves, but that the Buddha is not a savior except in the sense of being a teacher.[3]

What is the Jodoshinshu position regarding this criticism? The key concept of Jodoshinshu is that Amida Buddha moves *towards us* and endows us with the cause for Enlightenment. This point is clarified in the Sutras (the words of the historical Buddha Shakyamuni) and in the commentaries of the Buddhist masters who transmitted the doctrinal tradition in India, China, and Japan.

Let us start by clarifying the characteristics of Buddhism and Jodoshinshu. Generally, Buddhism is a path followed by those striving to attain Enlightenment. Jodoshinshu, on the other hand, is the path followed by those who cannot strive towards Enlightenment. The two positions may seem poles apart, but they actually are not.

---

3   Sir Charles Eliot, *Japanese Buddhism* (London: Edward Arnold and Co., 1935), p. 360.

Buddhism is usually considered and defined around the life experience of Shakyamuni Buddha, who gave up the material life of a prince to attain Truth. The process leading to his Enlightenment is generally believed to be the one and only Buddhist way in most English translations of the sutras. Whenever Buddha-dharma is considered in the west, it is usually from that perspective.

Buddhism does not insist that we must strive to *attain Truth*, rather the emphasis is placed on *striving* itself; that is, the process of going from ignorance to Enlightenment. That, however, is only a part of the picture. Another view of Buddha-dharma begins from the point of Enlightenment, and that is the perspective of Jodoshinshu.

Shakyamuni Buddha faced a very perplexing problem upon attaining Enlightenment. He realized that the nature of his Enlightenment experience could not be described in words. He therefore had to decide whether to keep the experience of Enlightenment to himself or to share it with others, even if he could not state exactly what the nature of his experience was. Moved by his great heart of Compassion, he could not refrain from sharing his experience, knowing full well that it could easily be misunderstood.

Shakyamuni Buddha sought out his former fellow ascetics who had renounced him for giving up the practice of self-mortification, and revealed the Truth to them as best he could. Here, we see the Compassion of Buddhahood moving towards those in ignorance and delusion. This is where the concept of Other-Power, Buddha's Power, or "merit-transference," is found.

Only because he had attained Enlightenment, was Shakyamuni Buddha able to perceive the capabilities of human beings. Some are able to leave home and family to seek the Truth as he did. But there are also those—indeed, the vast majority—who are tightly bound to home, family and relations and are unable to do so. For these people, the possibility of attaining Enlightenment through the monastic tradition of self-effort, is virtually nonexistent. Taking into account our human frailties, Shakyamuni Buddha offered the way to Enlightenment by the Buddha's-Power of Compassion symbolized by Amida Buddha.

Many sutras point out the Self-Power way of striving that is emphasized by what is considered Early Buddhism, but many other sutras stress the Other-Power way.

Jodoshinshu is based on three sutras. They are called the *Three Pure Land Sutras (Jodo Sambukkyo)*. The first sutra is the *Larger Sutra on the Buddha of Infinite Life*, *Larger Sutra* for short *(Daimuryojukyo)*. This sutra tells how Amida Buddha established and fulfilled Forty-eight Vows to lead all sentient beings to Enlightenment.[4]

The second sutra is the *Sutra on Meditation on the Buddha of Infinite Life (Kanmuryojukyo)*. This sutra describes our human capacities and how we can realize the Land of Enlightenment (the Pure Land) through Amida Buddha's Compassion.[5]

The third sutra is the *Amida Sutra (Amidakyo)*, often called the *Smaller Sutra* to contrast it with the *Larger Sutra*. This sutra describes the Land of Enlightenment and how it can be realized.[6]

The *Three Pure Land Sutras* combine to describe how Amida Buddha works and moves towards us.

The teaching of Buddha's-Power was further developed by the Seven Masters of Jodoshinshu. All seven began their Buddhist practice in the monastic tradition of Self-Power.

---

4   *Shinshu Shogyo Zensho*, Vol I, (Kyoto, Kyoshoin, 1958) p. 1-47. Henceforth referred to as *SSZ*

5   Ibid., pp. 48-66

6   Ibid., pp. 67-72.

Eventually, however, they adopted and taught the way of Buddha's-Power.

The first master was Nagarjuna of India (c. 2nd-3rd Century A.D.). He developed the Madyamika (Middle Way) School of Buddhist philosophy. For followers of Jodoshinshu, however, his greatest work was clarifying the difference between the Difficult Path and the Easy Path. The Difficult Path refers to the way of Self-Power and the Easy Path refers to the path of uttering Amida Buddha's Name with a faithful mind.[7] This is explained in the section titled *Chapter on Easy Practice (Igyobon)* of a work called *Commentary on the First Two Stages of the Ten Stages (Jujubibasharon)*.

The second master was Vasubandhu of India (c. 5th Century A.D.). He was a brilliant philosopher of Buddhism and is best known for the Yogacara "Consciousness Only" school of Buddhist philosophy. This school holds that all phenomena, whether mental or material, are reducible to one's basic consciousness called "consciousness-store"). In his *Discourse on the Pure Land (Jodoron)* however, Vasubandhu explained the importance of *single-minded shinjin* in Amida Buddha for realization of the Pure Land of Peace and Bliss.[8]

The third master was T'an-luan of China (476-645 A.D.). He was a brilliant scholar of the *Four Abhidharma School (Shiron)*, which studies the discourses dealing with the higher or special Dharma. In his *Commentary on the Discourse on the Pure Land (Ojoronchu)*, he clarified the concept of Other-Power. He makes it clear that realization of the Pure Land is due solely to Amida Buddha's Vow.[9]

---

7   Ibid., p. 254.
8   Ibid., p. 269.
9   Ibid., pp. 347-348.

The fourth master was Tao-cho of China (562-645). He was an exponent of the Emptiness (*Sunyata*) philosophy who later converted to the Pure Land teaching. In his *A Collection of Passages Concerning the Land of Bliss (Anrakushu)*, Tao-cho divided the teaching of Shakyamuni Buddha into the Sacred Path and the Pure Land Path. The former is the difficult way and the latter is the easy way. He developed the meaning of *Nembutsu* (uttering the name of Amida Buddha).[10]

The fifth master was Shan-tao of China (613-681). He was a strong advocate of the message found in the *Sutra on Meditation on the Buddha of Infinite Life (Kanmuryojukyo)*. In his *Commentary on the Kanmuryojukyo (Kangyosho)*, he pointed out that common mortals could attain Enlightenment by virtue of the Vow and Practice embodied in the Nembutsu.[11]

The sixth master was Genshin of Japan (942-1017). He was a master of the Tendai School and of the Pure Land teaching. In his *A Collection of Essential Passages Concerning Birth in the Pure Land (Ojoyoshu)*, he tossed aside all pretense at learning, saying that the teaching of the Pure Land was the only way to Enlightenment in the world and time in which he lived.[12]

The seventh master was Genku of Japan (1133-1212), better known to us as Honen. He was Shinran Shonin's personal teacher. In his *A Collection of Passages Concerning the Nembutsu of the Best Selected Original Vow (Senjakushu)*, Honen clarified the importance of uttering the Name of Amida Buddha.[13]

---

10   Ibid., p. 406.
11   Ibid., p. 534.
12   Ibid., p. 729.
13   Ibid., p. 936.

All Seven Masters began their search for Enlightenment by following the Self-Power tradition and monastic life-style. But each was also concerned about those who, either through lack of ability or circumstances in their life, could not follow the rigorous Buddhist meditative practices that are prescribed.

As Shinran Shonin studied the words of Shakyamuni Buddha and the Seven Masters, he realized that a foolish being like himself, with all his ties to human existence, could attain Enlightenment only through Other-Power. He wrote:

> If the single thought of joy is awakened in one's mind,
> Though passions are not severed, he will attain Nirvana.
> When ordinary men, sages, grave sinners, and abusers of the Dharma are all converted,
> They are like various waters turned into one in taste on entering the sea.[14]

The above is a brief description of how Jodoshinshu developed and how it fits into the tradition of Buddhism. Eliot is correct in one respect, however. He looks at Buddhism through the teaching and life-style of the historical Buddha Shakyamuni, who only points the way to Enlightenment. The responsibility of his followers is to strive along the way he pointed out. From this viewpoint we can understand why Eliot does not feel Jodoshinshu is an authentic Buddhist teaching.

Actually, however, Jodoshinshu is much broader in its viewpoint because the emphasis is not exclusively on the historical Shakyamuni Buddha. Rather, emphasis is placed on the *content* of the Buddha's Enlightenment; that is,

---

14   Shinran, *RTS, Shoshinge,* (Kyoto, 1961), p. 23.

Enlightenment with the virtues of Wisdom and Compassion which are transferred to us who dwell in delusion so that we may awaken to Truth. In other words, Jodoshinshu stresses the work of Enlightenment in its ultimate form.

Jodoshinshu is thus based on the dynamic motion of Enlightenment as it moves to enlighten us. Since that is also the goal of Buddhism in general, the conclusion cannot be other than that Jodoshinshu is an authentic Buddhist teaching.

The main reason Eliot did not realize that Jodoshinshu is an authentic Buddhist teaching is because he misunderstood the relationship between Shakyamuni Buddha and Amida Buddha. Shakyamuni Buddha is often considered the historical Buddha and Amida Buddha the spiritual Buddha. What is the relationship between them?

Shakyamuni Buddha and Amida Buddha

Two things are necessary to guide us in bettering ourselves. The first is clarity or objectivity, and the second is
warmth or subjectivity. Clarity means that things must be
seen in their proper context. This can be called wisdom,
knowledge, or "seeing the light."

But clarity is not enough. We must also have warmth and
subjectivity to complement it. Warmth is what moves us
and urges us to share wisdom in a responsible manner. It
gives sense to our lives.

Both clarity and warmth are necessary to live meaning-
fully. They help us to share the clarity that we see, and also
to help others see the light. Warmth can be called compassion that gives life to clarity.

Our world will not mean much without clarity and
warmth. Clarity-wisdom and warmth-compassion give us
courage, responsibility, faith, and a sense of grateful joy.

Where does this clarity-wisdom and warmth-compassion
come from? They are given to us by others through our life
experiences. In Jodoshinshu, clarity-wisdom and warmth-
compassion are the Wisdom and Compassion of Enlightenment. In this case, "given to us by others" means that

shinjin is given by the Compassion of Amida Buddha/Other-Power.

Let us clarify the meaning of Amida Buddha, who perfected and fulfilled the Light and Life of Universal Wisdom and Compassion. Shinran Shonin designated the Twelfth of Amida Buddha's Forty-eight Vows as the "Vow of Infinite Light" and the Thirteenth Vow as the "Vow of Infinite Life."[15]

The Twelfth Vow is:

> If, after attaining Buddhahood, my light should be limited and not shine upon a hundred *kotis* of *nayutas* of Buddha Lands, may I not attain the Perfect Enlightenment.[16]

The Thirteenth Vow is:

> If after attaining Buddhahood, my life should be measurable and limited to a hundred *kotis* of *nayutas* of *kalpas*, may I not attain the Perfect Enlightenment.[17]

Buddhahood, Light and Life, and Wisdom and Compassion are words that refer to the contents of Enlightenment. Amida Buddha, being the embodiment of Wisdom-Light and Compassion-Life, is a Buddha who manifests the meaning of Ultimate Enlightenment. In Jodoshinshu, therefore, Amida Buddha does the ultimate work of Compassion. The work of this Compassionate Buddha is to awaken us to the Truth, regardless of our condition, circumstance, or capability. This working force of Compassion is referred to as Other-Power.

---

15   Shinran, *RTS Kyogyoshinsho*, p. 150.
16   Ibid., p. 152.
17   Ibid.

That is why Amida Buddha is the central object of worship in Jodoshinshu and why he is described in terms such as infinite, inconceivable, and immeasurable. Indeed, Amida Buddha is often called the "Buddha of Infinite-Inconceivable-Immeasurable Light" and "Infinite-Inconceivable-Immeasurable Life." These names indicate that Amida Buddha is beyond the time/space framework within which we live.

The word "Amida" is taken from the first part of the Japanese transliteration of two Sanskrit words, *Amitabha* and *Amitayus*, which are translated "limitless light" and "limitless life," respectively. *Amita* by itself means "limitless." In Buddhism, light symbolizes wisdom and life symbolizes compassion. In using words such as infinite, inconceivable, and immeasurable to describe Amida Buddha, we are attempting to express the essence of Enlightenment itself, which, of course, is actually impossible.

The problem is, how can we come to any conceptual understanding of the essence of Enlightenment when the only tools available to us are words, which by their very nature are limited, and therefore cannot be used to express the limitless.

Disillusioned and ignorant beings can never come to any awakening of this great Truth. We are so bound by delusion that we are incapable of seeing the Truth.

That is why we need a teacher who has attained Enlightenment, a teacher in the physical and historical realm who has attained Enlightenment and therefore can see the bonds of delusion. That teacher is Shakyamuni Buddha.

Shakyamuni Buddha was born Siddhartha Gautama. He lost his mother soon after birth, married, had a son, saw the sufferings of life, and sought the Truth. He attained Enlightenment after a long struggle. The content of his Enlightenment is twofold; 1) All-Knowing Wisdom; 2)

Dynamically Loving Compassion. In *Buddha, Truth, and Brotherhood*, it states:

> When Shakyamuni Buddha decided to break from the worldly life, he made four great vows: To save all people; to renounce all worldly desires; to learn all the teachings; and to attain perfect enlightenment. These vows did not originate with him—they were a manifestation of the love and compassion that is fundamental in the self-nature of Buddhahood.[18]

Moved by the Enlightenment that he attained, Shakyamuni Buddha taught the Dharma (the Truth) for forty-five years until his physical death. He then attained the Enlightened ideal of Amida, the embodiment of Wisdom and Compassion, which is eternal in its nature.

How does Shakyamuni Buddha exemplify the abstract concept of Infinite-Inconceivable-Immeasurable-Life-Compassion (which is what Amida Buddha is) so that we may understand? Through his own example, Shakyamuni Buddha placed Enlightenment in its proper context, and then demonstrated how it dynamically moves to awaken our minds and hearts. He pointed to Bodhisattvas as examples of Compassion in Action: the Bodhisattva strives for Buddhahood, but consciously stops one step away from it in order to bring all sentient beings to that same state. Shakyamuni Buddha accomplished two things in explaining the dynamic motion of Compassion in this manner.

First, he showed that the essence of Enlightenment is also the dynamic motion of Wisdom and Compassion.

Second, he showed that the dynamic motion of Enlightenment is completed by compassionately moving

---

18   *Buddha, Truth, and Brotherhood* (Santa Barbara: Dwight Goddard, 1934), p. 12.

towards all beings, awakening them to Truth, and endowing them with Enlightenment.

Shakyamuni Buddha clarified the uniqueness of Compassion by identifying the Bodhisattva as Dharmakara, meaning "treasury of merits." This name symbolizes the causal fulfillment of Amida Buddha's Enlightenment.

Finally, Shakyamuni Buddha explained the dynamic motion of Enlightenment through the process of cause and effect because cause and effect can be understood through our rational faculties.

The following description of Dharmakara Bodhisattva (Amida Buddha in his state of striving) is contained in the *Larger Sutra*. Once a king heard the teachings of the Buddha Lokesvararaja, felt great joy, and aspired to see the Truth (the Dharma). He abandoned his throne and his land, and became a mendicant.[19] He made Forty-eight Vows (cause) and fulfilled them after countless eons of practice (effect). The point of this story is that Enlightenment moves towards us. That is how Shakyamuni Buddha introduced the movement of Compassion within the sequence of cause and effect.

What is the significance of Dharmakara Bodhisattva's Forty-eight Vows? They indicate the basic spirit of Enlightenment that desires to lead everyone and everything to Enlightenment. The vows signify dynamic motion in all areas of concern. In the second half of the *Larger Sutra*, the vows are said to be fulfilled, thus showing that Enlightenment in terms of Wisdom and Compassion, is a moving process. The *Larger Sutra* teaches us that although Enlightenment is not a part of our nature, Wisdom and Compassion are what bring us to a true and meaningful life.

---

19   *SSZ*, Vol. I pp. 5-6.

Shakyamuni Buddha thus clarified the abstract concept of Enlightenment so that it has meaning for us. He showed that Enlightenment is truly inconceivable, immeasurable, infinite, and inexpressible because, from our standpoint, it is inconceivable that such an Infinite-Immeasurable-Inexpressible-Compassion should act for our sake. That is why Shinran Shonin rejoiced in *shinjin*. He wrote:

> How happy am I, Gutoku Shaku Shinran, to have been able to meet with the holy scriptures from India and the commentaries by Chinese and Japanese masters, which are difficult to meet, and to have been able to hear their teachings which are difficult to hear! In believing reverently in the Teaching, Practice, and Enlightenment of the True Teaching, I have realized particularly Amida Buddha's deep Benevolence. Hereupon, I express my joy over what I heard and praise what I have received.[20]

The relationship between Amida Buddha and Shakyamuni Buddha can be summarized as follows:

First, Amida Buddha symbolizes the Compassionate movement of Enlightenment towards sentient beings.

Second, Shakyamuni Buddha taught us about Amida Buddha.

Third, from the standpoint of Enlightenment, Amida Buddha and Shakyamuni Buddha are One.

Fourth, as a historical reference, Amida Buddha is the ideal towards which Shakyamuni Buddha strove. The ideal is termed Universal Wisdom and Compassion. Amida Buddha is the Enlightenment that Shakyamuni attained.

Because Shakyamuni Buddha had a physical body, he had the same needs as all human beings. His Enlightenment is therefore referred to as "Nirvana with residue." Only after

---

20   Shinran, *RTS, Kyogyoshinsho*, pp. 25-26.

passing on to *Parinirvana* (death), did he attain "Nirvana without residue."

We can also make the following statements in characterizing the roles of Amida Buddha, Shakyamuni Buddha, and Dharmakara Bodhisattva:

Amida Buddha is the embodiment of Wisdom and Compassion, the ultimate principle of dynamic Enlightenment.

Dharmakara Bodhisattva is a personified description of how Wisdom and Compassion—the ultimate principle of Enlightenment—dynamically moves in relation to us. The Forty-Eight Vows express the complexity of Buddha's dynamic motion and deep insight.

Shakyamuni Buddha was a human being who attained Enlightenment, and who explained the workings of Wisdom and Compassion so that we can understand.

Now, let us consider how the Compassionate Amida Buddha relates to us. The motion of Amida Buddha towards us is best described and clarified in terms of the Vows.

Vows and Their Significance

Vows (*Gan*) are very important in directing our lives. As an example, parents vow to love and provide for their children; students vow to study hard in order to succeed and get good grades; and even children vow or promise to be good. In short, vows indicate the direction, goals, desires, the maturity and responsibility that we feel.

As an example of the importance of vows, let us say someone wishes to help the sick, injured and weak. He or she vows to become a physician, investigates all avenues to be accepted into medical school, and then studies to perfect his or her knowledge and techniques of curing people. This can be called their practice in the causal state of becoming a physician. With the completion of their studies, that is, fulfillment of their vows, they are given the title of Physician. That title embodies all the virtues of their hard work and study, their trust of people, and their ability and concerns. He or she fulfills his or her vows by returning to the world of the sick, injured and weak as a physician.

Vows are important in leading others to Enlightenment. Generally, they indicate the reasons for a Buddha's practice. Their fulfillment is a manifestation of the ultimate desire to enlighten all beings and indicates how those beings will be

Enlightened. In short, vows symbolize the working of Compassion. From a causal standpoint, vows proclaim the untiring effort of a Bodhisattva to enlighten all beings. More importantly, the fulfilled vows indicate the dynamic motion of the Compassionate Buddha moving towards all beings.

Shakyamuni Buddha made Four Great Vows during his causal state. These vows are: to renounce all worldly desires, to learn all the teachings, to save all people, and to attain perfect Enlightenment. And he attained Enlightenment because he fulfilled all his vows.

In Jodoshinshu, Amida Buddha is considered to have made and fulfilled Forty-eight Vows. These vows indicate who, why, what, and how all beings in the universe will be led to Enlightenment. The universality of the vows indicate the greatness of Amida Buddha's Compassion. However, special significance is given to the Eighteenth Vow, which is called the Original Vow (*Hongan*), or the vow that deals with the awakening of *shinjin* in us through the Compassion of Other-Power. Shinran Shonin wrote:

> As I contemplate matters, I see that the acquirement of Serene *shinjin* arises out of Amida Buddha's Selected Vow, and that the awakening of the True Mind is made possible by the compassionate and skillful means of the Great Sage (Shakyamuni Buddha).[21]

The Eighteenth Vow states that if we awaken to *shinjin* and utter the Name, we will unfailingly be born in the Pure Land of Enlightenment.[22] In the passage concerning the fulfillment of the vow, it is said that Birth in the Pure Land

---

21   Shinran, *RTS, Kyogyoshinsho*, p. 84.
22   Ibid., p. 90.

of Enlightenment is made possible by hearing Amida Buddha's Name and having joy in *shinjin* through the Buddha's sincere endowment.[23] This vow is Amida Buddha's proclamation that although our nature is ignorance and evil, we can attain Birth in the Pure Land because of the dynamic motion of Amida Buddha's Compassion.

Questions still remain however, how does Amida come in contact with us? To understand this, we must consider the Name (*Myogo,*—the Name-that-Calls). In Jodoshinshu, the work of the Name is also known as the Great Practice (*Daigyo*).

---

23 Ibid., p. 90.

Name: Great Practice

Names are very important. A person's name can be said to identify that person's character, virtues, attitudes, capabilities, promise, and countless other things, whether good or bad. Certainly it expresses the desires of parents for their child. A name can also be said to awaken respect in others. In time, that respect may develop into an unquestioned trust. That trust may further develop into praising that person's name. In praising that name, others will hear, realize the virtues implied, and also come to respect that person. All names, whether they identify a person or occupation, have this quality. For example, let us consider the name, "teacher." As people come in contact with a teacher's virtues, they will begin to praise that teacher's name, and as they listen, come to accept that he can help them attain knowledge.

The tie between Amida Buddha and us sentient beings is the Name, *Namoamidabutsu.* From Amida Buddha's standpoint, *Namoamidabutsu* is the "Name-that-calls" to awaken us to *shinjin.* From our standpoint, however, *Namoamidabutsu* is an expression of gratitude for being awakened to *shinjin.* Shinran Shonin says that the Name is used because it is easy to hold in our mind and easy for an ignorant person to say.[24]

Amida Buddha's Name is the crystallization of all the practices accomplished and virtues accumulated for the sake of our birth in the Pure Land. Shinran Shonin says the Name was perfected because of Amida Buddha's innumerable practices.[25] That is why it is the cause for our Birth in the Pure Land and subsequent Enlightenment there. Because all the virtues of the Buddha are embodied within the Name, utterance of the Name in gratitude (Nembutsu) is the true expression of gratitude for *shinjin*. That is why the Compassionate work of the Name is also known as the Great Practice of the Other Power. Shinran Shonin wrote:

> This Practice (reciting the Name) embodies all good and contains all virtues. It enables sentient beings to attain the all-complete merits very quickly, and is the treasure-sea of the virtues of True Thusness, or One Truth. Hence, it is called the Great Practice.[26]

Receiving the Name is referred to as *shinjin*. When *shinjin* is received, the Name comes out spontaneously and is referred to as "uttering the Name." In other words, the Name is the source of *shinjin* and Utterance.

But if *shinjin* and Utterance are awakened in us by the Great Practice of the Name, then what is there for us to do? Do we have to do anything to be worthy of receiving *shinjin*? That is the subject of the next section.

---

24 *RTS, Tannisho* (Kyoto, 1966), p. 39
25 Shinran, *Passages on the Pure Land Way, Shin Buddhist Translation Series*, (Hongwanji International Center, Kyoto, 1982), p. 29. Henceforth referred to as *SBTS*.
26 *RTS, Kyogyoshinsho*, p. 40.

The Meaning of Practice

The two ways in which we attain a goal are through self-effort and through other's-effort. In self-effort, the emphasis is on what we do ourselves. That is our practice. If you graduate from school with good grades, you probably feel, "I did it!" The point of reference for that statement is the study or practice you put in. This is known as Self-Power (*Jiriki*) in Jodoshinshu.

In other's-effort, the emphasis is on what someone else does to make our accomplishments possible. If you graduate from school with good grades, you could credit the help of your teachers, parents, and all others who made it possible. Your inner feeling would be, "They made it possible!" With this feeling there is a great sense of gratitude. This is known as the way of Other-Power (*Tariki*), and is the viewpoint Shinran Shonin expanded and developed as the basis for the Jodoshinshu teaching.

In Jodoshinshu, *shinjin* is awakened in us by the Compassionate Great Practice of the Name. That is why we do not have to do anything in order to awaken it. But even more to the point, we cannot awaken *shinjin* through our own efforts even if we wanted to. If we try to attain *shinjin* through own efforts we will only find ourselves going around in circles. Trying to attain *shinjin* through our own efforts is like trying to "lift ourselves up by our own bootstraps." It is impossible because the person trying to do the lifting is also the person being lifted. That is why the emphasis in Jodoshinshu is placed on the Great Practice which awakens us to *shinjin* and Utterance of the Name, which is a position outside of ourselves.

Shinran Shonin wrote:

> Therefore, I know clearly that this Nembutsu practice is not the practice of self-power by common men and sages. Hence, it is called the "practice of non-merit-transference." The sages of Mahayana (Great Vehicle) and Hinayana (Small Vehicle) and the evil persons with delusions, whether heavy or light, should all equally take refuge in the great treasure-sea of the Selected Vow and attain Buddhahood through the Nembutsu.[27]

The only difficulty with this point of view is in simply accepting it. In our society, the tendency is, "Doing our own thing." In doing our own thing, however, we are very likely to fall into the trap of selfishness. How can we free ourselves from that predicament? If we are initially ignorant, how do we attain knowledge through our own efforts? That is our plight.

We must trust in others to help us. The only way we can attain the joy of knowledge is to trust others who share their knowledge with us. When that happens, we will realize two things. First, that we cannot realize greater knowledge through our own limited knowledge. Second, only through compassionate sharing by others can we come to a joyous realization of the truth. We need others to guide us and awaken to meaning and inspiration within us.

---

27   *RTS, Kyogyoshinsho, p.* 53.

The term "practice" is difficult for many followers of Jodoshinshu to understand. Let me clarify its meaning as traditionally understood in Buddhism in general and as it is understood in Jodoshinshu.

Practice usually means "to act and advance towards a goal." Actually, any action that leads to Enlightenment can be called practice. The historical and traditional reference for practice is found in the actions of Shakyamuni Buddha as he sought Enlightenment. In other words, practice is what we do in attempting to go from ignorance to Enlightenment. Practices include meditation; the *Six Paramitas* (Perfections) of Giving, Morality, Patience, Vigor, Concentration, and Wisdom; the *Eight-fold Path* of Right View, Right Thought, Right Speech, Right Conduct, Right Livelihood, Right Effort, Right Mindfulness, and Right Concentration; renunciation of the household life to enter a monastery; and so on. These are the "practices" traditionally performed by Buddhists in order to attain Enlightenment.

Many kinds of practices developed as the Pure Land teaching was transmitted from India, to China, and then to Japan, but the emphasis was placed on reciting the Buddha's Name, *Namoamidabutsu*. Shan-tao, the fifth master of Jodoshinshu from China, regarded reciting the Buddha's Name as the Act of Right Assurance for Birth in the Pure Land.[28] Following Shan-tao's teaching, Honen Shonin, the seventh master of Jodoshinshu, called the Eighteenth Vow, the Vow of Attaining Birth Through the Nembutsu.[29] Many different understandings regarding the practice of reciting the Buddha's Name developed, but they can be divided into the two main streams previously men-

---

28 *SSZ* Vol. I, p. 538.
29 Ibid., p. 947.

tioned: the practice of Self-Power and reliance on Other-Power.

Shinran Shonin revealed the true significance of the Nembutsu by clarifying the concept of Great Practice, which refers to the dynamic motion of Amida Buddha, or in the causal sense, the practice of Dharmakara Bodhisattva and his fulfillment of the Seventeenth Vow. This Vow declares that the Name, *Namoamidabutsu*, will be praised by all the Buddhas in the ten directions (north, south, west, east, northeast, southeast, northwest, northeast, up, and down).[30] In other words, everywhere in space. According to Shinran Shonin, the Seventeenth Vow stresses two major points.

The first point is that the Buddha's Name, *Namoamidabutsu*, contains the ultimate meaning of Wisdom and Compassion (Enlightenment). *Namoamidabutsu* is the key to the process of Enlightenment for those who cannot comprehend the meaning of Enlightenment.

The second point is that because the Buddha's Name is Wisdom and Compassion itself, all Buddhas in the ten quarters praise *Namoamidabutsu*. The Name can thus be heard everywhere by anyone. Because the Name is the ultimate expression of Enlightenment, and because it is praised by all the Buddhas, its movement is towards us. Shinran Shonin identifies this with the working of the Great Practice based on the fulfillment passage of the Seventeenth Vow. This Vow states that the Buddhas of the ten quarters, as numerous as the sands of the River Ganges, all praise the inconceivable, sublime merits of the Buddha of Infinite Life and Infinite Light.[31] Shakyamuni Buddha gives testimony to the Great Practice which leads all beings to Enlighten-

---

30   Ibid., p. 9. Quoted by Shinran, *RTS, Kyogyoshinsho*, p. 41.
31   Ibid., p. 24. Quoted by Shinran, *RTS, Kyogyoshinsho*, p. 42.

ment by making this statement about the Compassion of Amida Buddha. By referring to the virtuous practice of Amida Buddha, Shakyamuni Buddha praised the merits and virtues of the Buddha of Infinite Life and Infinite Light. Because Bodhisattva Dharmakara made the Forty-eight Vows and fulfilled them in the Name of Amida Buddha, this movement is called Great Practice. It describes how Enlightenment moves in relation to us.

The reason "practice" is not stressed in Jodoshinshu is because we, as householders, cannot perform the traditional monastic practices for Enlightenment because of our jobs, having to care for our parents, children, and all the responsibilities that householders have. Monks and nuns perform practices in hopes of attaining Enlightenment. Because their actions are based on self-seeking and self-centeredness, however, their actions tend to increase their selfishness. Shinran Shonin recognized this futile and limited nature of human endeavor. That is why the emphasis of Jodoshinshu is placed on the Great Practice of Amida Buddha who awakens *shinjin* in those of us who cannot follow the practices of monastic Buddhism.

Practice is also not considered nor generally discussed because Jodoshinshu does not acknowledge any Self-Powered practice as a method for attaining Enlightenment. Jodoshinshu does however, consider Utterance of the Name as the Great Practice. That is, when the true significance of the Great Practice is awakened in our minds as *shinjin*, the Name is uttered spontaneously and that utterance is termed the Great Practice. Shinran Shonin interprets uttering the Name as Great Practice because it does not originate from a conscious effort on our part, but rather, is the result of Amida Buddha's Compassionate Work.[32] In other words, our utterance is not separate from the Great Practice of Amida Buddha. In this regard, continuing to utter the Name is considered an expression of gratitude to Buddha. Not only uttering the Name, but other activities such as chanting sutras and meditation that are considered "practices" in other Buddhist traditions, are considered to be expressions of gratitude in Jodoshinshu.

Those seeking *shinjin* perform other kinds of practices in addition to the Practice manifested by Other Power. Because Jodoshinshu presents it's teaching based on Other Power, attaining *shinjin* should not be difficult, and yet many people seem to feel it is. Confronted by the elusive *shinjin*, we feel the need to *do something*, even though we may know intellectually that trying to attain it puts our efforts in the category of Self-Power.

What kind of practice can we perform? We cannot perform the practices of the monastic tradition, but there is a practice, as an educational process, that we can perform to focus our direction. This practice is not the same as a practice to attain Enlightenment, but it does give us a view of ourselves and our condition. And that view is what can lead us to Amida Buddha and the awakening of *shinjin*.

Shinran Shonin performed the traditional Buddhist practices for twenty years on Mt. Hiei (the center for Buddhist learning in Japan at that time). He struggled with the conflicts between his intellectual understanding and his physical passions and desires. This struggle arose while he was actively engaged in traditional Buddhist practices as a monk. And because of this conflict, Shinran Shonin felt he

---

32   *RTS, Kyogyoshinsho*, p. 40.

was actually moving further from Enlightenment rather than closer to it.

When he abandoned the monastic practices on Mt Hiei, sought guidance from Honen Shonin, and finally experienced *shinjin*, Shinran Shonin was able to review the course of his life and humbly admit that his realization of *shinjin* was solely due to the Compassionate Heart of Amida Buddha. In looking back, he saw that it was the working of Great Compassion, even in the darkness of his own impure and futile practice, that resulted in his *shinjin*. He therefore declared:

> Those who have received the True Practice and *shinjin* have much joy in their minds; hence, this state is called the Stage of Joy.[33]

Only then was Shinran Shonin able to comprehend the meaning of Great Practice. We must clearly understand that the Great Practice of Amida Buddha can be viewed only from the state of *shinjin*. The whole of Jodoshinshu stands upon this one point.

That was how Shinran Shonin was led to *shinjin*, but what about us? We are not in a position to follow the traditional monastic practices. We are householders bound to the things of this world. Even if we were guided to the Nembutsu, we would not have the joy and understanding of Great Practice. In fact, we are apt to struggle with miscellaneous practices in order to attain *shinjin*. Let us consider the utterance of the Nembutsu in this light.

With each utterance of the Buddha's Name, we are afforded the opportunity to see ourselves as we really are in relation to the Name that we are utter. We come to see, understand and feel where we stand. It is a learning process.

---

33   Ibid., p. 54.

As we begin to see ourselves in true perspective, a conflict may arise between the self and uttering the Name. And as we begin rejecting the Nembutsu, we find difficulty in uttering it. Our ego will not set us free. Nonetheless, it will eventually dawn on us that the Nembutsu is not something of our own convenience. In this realization, we find ourselves suspended between a state of egolessness on the one hand, and total ego on the other. Yet, joy wells up from deep within, and the Nembutsu begins to flow freely. In looking back, there is the realization that it was all due to the Compassionate Heart of Amida Buddha's Great Practice.

Stated in another way, Jodoshinshu does not recognize any self-powered practice as true practice. But when viewed from the standpoint of *shinjin*, even impure and futile practices are recognized as the Buddha's Compassionate Working. For example, we have to study, search, and strive to understand ourselves, our circumstances, and the power of Amida Buddha which can lead us to endowed *shinjin*. Yet this process of learning may lead to further questions, and rather than advancing to our goal, we may very likely go in the opposite direction. This process is considered to be significant in Jodoshinshu because through it we are made aware of the futility of our efforts and made to realize the Great Practice of the Other Power. This realization is the awakening to *shinjin*. Misdirected practice is thus accepted as an educational process that leads to *shinjin*.

Because the experience of *shinjin* is due to the Compassion of Amida Buddha, the entire dynamic experience is referred to as, "due to the Great Practice of Amida Buddha."

We must never forget that we are householders with all the problems of secular living. As a consequence, it is only natural that Jodoshinshu practice differs from the practices of monastic Buddhism. Further, because we are householders bound by ties to our loved ones, family and work, the way to Enlightenment is most easily received by relying on the Great Compassion and Great Practice of Amida Buddha. Only in this manner, can we "act and advance to a goal" in the attainment of Enlightenment.

But how do we receive the Name and thus awaken to *shinjin* and Utterance of the Name? This is the most crucial area of consideration in Shinran Shonin's teaching.

Shinjin: Daishin

Shinjin is often translated as "faith" and *daishin* as "great faith," but together, the words signify "the awakened, true and real mind." As we search for meaning in our lives, we constantly experience awakening through hearing. That is, hearing a word or a name can awaken us to a realization that gives meaning to our lives. For example, let us take the names of people or friends who give advice. If we did not know their reputation, we probably would not seek their advice. We would be skeptical. If, however, we heard others praise them, their virtues and abilities, then we would be more apt to listen to them. When the sincerity and virtue of a person frees us of any doubt, that is when we entrust ourselves to him or her.

Shinjin is the state in which the true and real mind of Amida Buddha (the Name) is awakened in us. The Name thus becomes the source of our *shinjin*, which is the right cause for our Birth in the Pure Land of Enlightenment. But, how is the awakening of *shinjin* possible?

As previously stated, the virtues of the Name are praised by innumerable Buddhas in the ten directions. By hearing the virtues of the Name, we experience the joyous awakening of *shinjin*. In other words, the instant we truly "hear," we are endowed with the virtues of the Name. The key then, is "hearing," which is identical with *shinjin*. But we cannot truly hear if we have doubts and self-assertions. Our minds must be free. The Name frees our minds because of its virtues. That is why awakening to *shinjin* is referred to as the "no doubt mind."[34] And with that awakening we are assured of Birth in the Pure Land of Enlightenment.

Shinjin is awakened when we hear the Great Practice of the Name as shown in the fulfillment passage of the Eighteenth Vow. *Shinjin* is also referred to as Great Shinjin (*Daishin*). Shinran Shonin wrote:

> If the ever-sinking common mortals, relying on the merit-transference of the Vow-Power and hearing the True Virtues, attain the supreme *shinjin*, then they attain Great Joy and the state of assurance (for Birth). Without cutting their passions and desires they instantly attain the Great Nirvana.[35]

Translating the word *shinjin* as "faith," has created much confusion. According to Shinran Shonin, *shinjin* is the "true (*shin*) mind (*jin*)" of Amida Buddha. He states that we do not have the true and real mind, and that is why the true and real mind of Amida Buddha awakens us. When we are filled with the realization of Amida Buddha's true and real mind, we become persons of *shinjin*. *Shinjin* also has the meaning of "to entrust." That is, as we become aware of our foolish selves, we realize the need for Amida Buddha's Compassion. Saying "*Namoamidabutsu*" (I entrust myself to Amida Buddha), expresses the fact that we realize Amida Buddha's Compassionate Work.

---

34 Ibid., p. 112.
35 *SSZ* Vol. II, p. 454.

We must take an honest account of the Jodoshinshu position in Buddhism in general in order to clarify *shinjin*. Where does Jodoshinshu stand in the history of Buddhism? Jodoshinshu clearly is not part of the traditional Buddhist Order. We have been considered householder Buddhists since the time of Shakyamuni Buddha,. This means that we are bound to family ties with all its frustrations, problems and joys, which do not help us in the traditional concept of Enlightenment. We are followers of Shakyamuni Buddha in a home setting. Our time spent on Buddhist practice is limited, if any time is spent at all. For householder Buddhists, there is only one way Enlightenment can be attained, and that is the way of *shinjin*. In other words, *shinjin* is awakened in us while we are in the midst of our problems. It is impossible for us to bring about the cause and effect of Enlightenment because of our family circusmstances..

Although Shinran Shonin stated that *shinjin* is the cause, *shinjin* is not caused by us. Rather, the cause is awakened in us by Amida Buddha. The Truth enlightens us because it is real and leaves no room for doubt. Accordingly, this *shinjin* is called the *True Shinjin*, *Pure Shinjin*, or *Great Shinjin*.

Without Amida Buddha working through the process of the Name, we cannot experience the awakened cause of *shinjin*.

Yet with all this emphasis on *shinjin* in Jodoshinshu, what, after all, is s*hinjin*? This question can be answered in two ways: intellectually and experientially. An intellectual answer will never be completely satisfactory because such an answer can only point the way. Because of the limitations of words, *shinjin*, as the true nature of Enlightenment can never be expressed in words. In the final analysis, *shinjin* must be a dynamic, personal experience which takes in our entire being. The gate of *shinjin* opens differently for each of us because we all have individual differences. And yet, all that can be presented in a booklet is an intellectual explanation of *shinjin*. With this in mind, let us consider *shinjin* from an intellectual standpoint.

First, Shinran Shonin firmly and objectively states that *shinjin* is what is endowed upon us by the Compassionate Amida Buddha through the dynamic process of his vows. *Shinjin* is not awakened in us by ourselves. The direction in which *shinjin* approaches is Amida Buddha to me.

Second, *shinjin* is traditionally understood as a realization that the bonds, ties and circumstances of our lives pull us away from Enlightenment, and that we can attain Enlightenment only through the Compassion of Amida Buddha. These are the two aspects that are felt in the realization of *shinjin*.

How did Shinran Shonin experience *shinjin*? He felt himself *moving away* from Enlightenment when he said:

> Truly I know. Sad is it that I, Gutoku Ran (Ignorant Short-haired One), sunk in the vast sea of lust and lost in the great mountain of desire for fame and profit, do not rejoice in joining the group of the Rightly Established State, nor do I enjoy coming near to the True Enlightenment. What a Shame! What a sorrow![36]

Here Shinran Shonin expresses what he really is, a man moved by passions and desires. He is tied down by the problems of living, bound by selfishness, and realizes he cannot attain Enlightenment by his own efforts. In other words, he views his condition and himself with complete honesty. Because of the Compassion of Amida Buddha, however, even a person like himself can be endowed with *shinjin*. That is why he continues:

---

36   *RTS, Kyogyoshinsho*, p. 132.

What a joy to place my mind in the soil of the
Buddha's Universal Vow and let my thoughts flow
into the sea of the Inconceivable Dharma! I deeply
acknowledge the Tathagata's (Amida Buddha's)
Compassion and sincerely appreciate the master's
benevolence in instructing me. As my joy increases,
my feeling of indebtedness grows deeper.[37]

Shinran Shonin savored the joys of *shinjin* because of
Amida Buddha's Great Compassion. At the same time, he
realized the great debt he owed, not only to Amida Buddha,
but to all those who compassionately guided and pointed
out the way.

Shinjin is the coming together of Amida Buddha and our
total being. In the experience of *shinjin,* we find ourselves
so overwhelmed by inconceivable Compassion that mind
and heart exist in a single instant of selflessness. It is an
instance in which we freely experience the total weight of
our karmic being of selfishness, as well as the joys of being
freed by the Compassion of Amida Buddha. It is a moment-
less moment that words cannot describe. It is a moment
known simply as *shinjin.*

Let us now consider an aspect of the Nembutsu that is a
natural outgrowth of the awakening to *shinjin*, that is, the
Name as an expression of gratitude.

---

37   Ibid., p. 211.

Utterance of the Name (Nembutsu)
Expression of Gratitude

If a friend sacrifices his time to help us in a crisis, we acknowledge that person and all that he did through saying his name. With that experience, a number of very important thoughts flood our minds and hearts whenever we think of that name.

First, we feel that the sacrifice took much time and effort.

Second, we realize that we would have been unable to get through the crisis without that person. Only because of that person were we able to survive.

Third, we feel humble with the realization that we have such a friend.

Fourth, we feel the inconceivable nature of our relationship. That is, we cannot help but wonder how, in this vast universe, we were able to meet such a person.

These are a few of the thoughts that we might have, and we say our friends name in gratitude precisely because we have such thoughts.

The realization of these feelings in relation to Amida Buddha's Great Compassion is called *shinjin*. The natural utterance of the Name in gratitude is called Nembutsu. Shinran Shonin says, "The true *shinjin* is necessarily accomplished by uttering the Name."[38]

Uttering the Name spontaneously follows the awakening to *shinjin*. Generally, the utterance is an expression of gratitude for being endowed with *shinjin* and being assured of Birth in the Pure Land of Enlightenment.

We often believe that utterance of the Name is our own doing, but that is not so. Actually, all the virtues contained in *shinjin* are through the Compassion of Amida Buddha. Those virtues are embodied in the Name and not in our utterance of it. But because the virtues are embodied in the Name, our grateful utterance has the power to embrace other beings still caught in delusion.

Utterance of the Name is thus the result of the awakened *shinjin*, bestowed upon us by the Compassionate Buddha through the fulfilled Eighteenth Vow. With the awakening to *shinjin*, we are assured of Birth in the Pure Land of Enlightenment.

Let us continue by discussing what is meant by Birth in the Pure Land.

---

38   Ibid., p. 112..

Birth in the Pure Land:
True Enlightenment

Attaining the Ultimate Goal

Whether we are aware of it or not, we all strive towards an ultimate goal. We should know therefore that we have a goal, and further, strive towards the highest goal that we can conceive. In order to attain that goal however, we must make an effort towards it. Yet, even as we strive, we are sustained by a vast network of interrelationships that allow us to strive towards that goal. This process can be called a case of "self-attainment is Other-attainment."

As an example, let us say someone wishes to become a teacher. He or she may study very hard, but without the help of teachers, students, books, and countless other things and people, will be unable to attain that goal. And it does not end there. The ever-widening interrelationships continue to enable us to fulfill the ultimate meaning of our lives.

The ultimate goal in Jodoshinshu is Birth in the Pure Land-True Enlightenment which results from *shinjin*. With the awakening to *shinjin* we are assured of two things: 1) The cause for Enlightenment in this life and,

2) Assurance of Birth in the Pure Land with the end of our
life in this world.

According to Shinran Shonin, Birth in the Pure Land
means attaining Nirvana (ultimate fulfillment) and becoming a Buddha. Of the Forty-eight Vows of Amida Buddha,
the Eleventh Vow[39] verifies our True Enlightenment;

> If upon my attaining Buddhahood, all beings and
> devas who are born in my country were not to abide
> in the country of those who have attained the right
> definite assurance and ultimately realize Nirvana, may
> I not attain the Supreme Enlightenment.

In Jodoshinshu, therefore, Birth in the Pure Land and
Buddhahood are simultaneous and are due solely to the
vow-power of Amida Buddha's Compassion. Those born
in the Pure Land attain the same Enlightenment as Amida
Buddha. Shinran Shonin says:

> Since depending on the Tathagata's pure Original
>   Vow
> We are born into the Pure Land of Birthlessness;
> Although we are originally of nine classes,
> There is not the distinction of even one or two.[40]

Still, we find it difficult to believe that we will be born in
the Pure Land because we are so evil. We cannot help
feeling that our Birth in that Serene Land will be hindered
if we do not remove the effects of our evil of the past, or at
the very least, stop creating evil now. But the unique point
of the Jodoshinshu teaching is that the conditional evil
that we find ourselves bound to, is not removed. Rather,
because Amida Buddha perfected all the conditions for our

---

39   Ibid, Vol. I, p. 9.
40   *RTS, Koso Wasan*, p. 69.

Enlightenment, our evil can be turned into virtue. According to Shinran Shonin:

> By the benefit of the Unhindered Light,
> The virtuous, great Shinjin is obtained;
> Assuredly does our evil passion turn into En-
>   lightenment
> As ice melts to water. [41]

That is why we find such apparently contradictory statements in Jodoshinshu as "Birth-and-death is Nirvana" and "Passion-and-desire is Bodhi."

These are very difficult concepts; however, they precisely describe our everyday life. For example, if we cannot remove our own ignorance, we may not even realize that we are ignorant. Those who do know, however, will not attempt to remove ignorance because ignorance is relative, and is not something that can be removed. All that a person can do is add knowledge to their being. As knowledge is added, we come to know. That is how we are able to go from ignorance to knowledge. Ignorance and knowledge are not separate parts of our being but an integral part of our very make-up. In this realization, "ignorance is knowledge," and "knowledge is ignorance." That is, ignorance is the basis for knowledge, and knowledge is an outgrowth of ignorance. Such statements indicate a realization that ignorance and knowledge are interrelated.

Considering the above, we can understand why Shinran Shonin expressed his heartfelt gratitude in the following manner:

---

41   Ibid, p. 62.

The benevolence of the Tathagata's great compassion,
Even if we must crush our bodies, should be returned in gratitude..
The benevolence of the masters and teachers,
Even if we must break our bodies, should be returned in gratitude..[42]

Let me clarify a point regarding Birth in the Pure Land-Enlightenment. Many are dissatisfied with the idea that Enlightenment is attained in the Pure Land only after death. Like Charles Eliot, such people reason that Buddhism stresses the concept of Enlightenment in this life so why must we wait until leaving this world?. To answer this question, let us consider certain basic points about what Buddhism means when referring to Enlightenment in this life.

First is the example of Shakyamuni Buddha, who left home, struggled, and finally attained the Truth. Those who strive for Enlightenment in this life generally follow a life-style similar to which the Buddha followed.

Second, those who try to emulate Shakyamuni Buddha, center their life around attaining the ideal. He or she joins a monastery, meditates, cuts ties with family, home, loved ones and society. The attachments to others and material things must be cut away or limited. When the Buddhist life is thus defined, it is possible to conceive of Enlightenment for the monk because those conditions make Enlightenment a possibility.

When Jodo Shinshu points to the way of Enlightenment in this life, however, it stresses *shinjin* for the following reasons:

---

42   Shinran, *RTS, Shozomatsu Wasan* (Ryukoku University, Kyoto, 1980), p. 59..

First, we are householders who must work to survive, provide and live. Our main concern is to support and maintain ourselves and our family. We are bound by all the problems of human existence. Rather than cut away or limit attachments, we allow them to grow. Or rather, we cannot help but make attachments grow.

Second, to follow the traditional practices is really a limited possibility for a householder whose life-style is such that the cause and effect of Enlightenment cannot be fulfilled by their efforts. That is why Amida Buddha's Great Compassion is required to awaken *shinjin* (the cause) so that Enlightenment (the effect) can take place within us.

Shinjin is what places us at the door of Enlightenment, and death (lack of physical desires) is what opens that door. That is the Jodoshinshu key to entering the Heart of Universal Wisdom and Compassion. Once we enter the door of Enlightenment, we will forever move with the Heart of Universal Wisdom and Compassion to embrace all beings in suffering. Considering our human condition, there is no other way possible. We must now discuss the ultimate goal; that is, the Pure Land.

Birth in the Pure Land Enlightenment

Our hope and dream is to attain the ultimate goal of joy, happiness and meaning in life.

In Jodoshinshu this goal is attained when we are born in the Pure Land. Unfortunately, the concept of the Pure Land has confused many, especially those born outside the Orient. What is the Pure Land and how are we to understand this "Land"?

The historical Shakyamuni Buddha described the Pure Land as follows:

> "The ground of the Buddha Country is made of nature's seven gems...the land is wide and extensive...superb is the beauty...pure and grand is the splendor...it has no parallel in all the worlds."[43]

This description of the Pure Land in terms of beauty, purity, and splendor goes far beyond what we see in our physical world, or indeed, even that world which we may imagine.

---

43   *SSZ* Vol. I, pp. 15-16.

But, what do all these words actually point to? At first glance, it seems that the Pure Land is all that this world is not; a heaven-like place to enjoy after the trials and tribulations of human existence. There is some truth in this kind of thinking. And such a Pure Land was probably taught by some teachers.

Actuality, however, the Pure Land is Enlightenment itself. It is the Land of Wisdom and Compassion. As Shinran Shonin says, "This Land is the Land of Immeasurable Light."[44]

In describing the nature of the Pure Land in the above words, Shinran Shonin is pointing to the Twelfth Vow (*Vow of Infinite Light*) and the Thirteenth Vow (*Vow of Infinite Life*). In other words, the Pure Land is composed of immeasurable Light and Life, which means infinite Wisdom and Compassion, the essence of Enlightenment. For this reason, the Pure Land, while it must be infinitely better than the world of our actual experience, is described in relation to those things that we can see. Shinran Shonin says:

> The adornments of the Land of Peace and Bliss
> Even by the Sakyan Sage, with unhindered elo-
> quence,
> Cannot be fully described, so says Shakyamuni
> Buddha.
> Take refuge in the Ineffable Buddha (Amida).[45]

To be desired and coveted, the "Land" must be pure in all respects. We already live in a world of suffering so we would not be attracted to a land where suffering exists. That is why the Pure Land is described in such idealistic terms. But, actually, what is really being described is En-

---

44   *RTS, Kyogyoshinsho*, p. 151.
45   Shinran, *RTS, Jodo Wasan* (Ryukoku Univ., Kyoto, 1965) p. 56..

lightenment itself (which is Wisdom-Light and Compassion-Life). Since the Pure Land is Enlightenment itself, it is understandable that there will be joy and happiness for those who attain it. The joy and happiness grow even greater because of the dynamic motion of Enlightenment that embraces all sentient beings in delusion and ignorance.

In Jodoshinshu, the Pure Land is also referred to as Nirvana (ultimate fulfillment). Let us clarify this point.

Nirvana: Ultimate Fulfillment

As we proceed through life, we constantly strive towards an "ultimate goal." For example, the ultimate goal of a medical student is to become a physician. He works, studies and strives towards that goal. Upon reaching his goal, however, he is faced with the "ultimate fulfillment" of actually being a physician—to cure and comfort the weak, sick and injured.

In the Buddha-dharma, we all strive towards the ultimate goal of Nirvana. It is a life-time endeavor because Nirvana is literally defined as "blowing out," or "extinguishing," passions and desires. Consequently, Nirvana is described as "ultimate peace," "tranquility," or "peaceful bliss."

In Jodoshinshu, the concept of Nirvana has been expanded to include the Mahayana concept of "benefiting-self and benefiting others." Through the Compassion of Amida Buddha, we attain the "self-benefit" of Birth in the Pure Land-Enlightenment, which simultaneously activates the work of "benefiting-others" still caught in the bonds of evil and delusion. Through the Compassion of Amida Buddha, we attain the ultimate goal of Birth in the Pure Land-Enlightenment, and at that very moment become One with Amida Buddha in order to lead others to Enlightenment. That is the ultimate fulfillment of Nirvana. And that is why Shinran Shonin called attainment in Jodoshinshu the "Great Nirvana which is the fruition stage of Teaching and Benefiting Others."[46]

With the "self-benefit" of Birth in the Pure Land-Enlightenment, the "phase of going" is completed.

Simultaneously with Birth in the Pure Land-Enlightenment, however, the "phase of returning" to "benefit-others" is manifested. This is the Jodoshinshu concept of Nirvana.

Finally, we need to clarify the meaning of the Phase of Going and the Phase of Returning, two aspects that exemplify the dynamic nature of Jodoshinshu.

---

46   *SBTS, Passages on the Pure Land Way.*

Phase of Going and Phase of Returning

We may think we strive towards a goal through our own efforts, but actually, we are being guided towards it by countless people and events. Through a teacher's compassion, we are taught to see the ways of life, receive guidelines on how to work, awaken to a sense of trust in the teacher, and thus understand how to live. With this understanding comes joy and gratitude for being guided to the goal. We then join hands with our teachers and strive to enlighten those still caught in the web of ignorance regarding how to truly live.

In Jodoshinshu, the concept of Merit-transference in the "phase of going" means that we are guided through the following process because of the Compassion of Amida Buddha: 1. Meeting with the teachings, 2. Being endowed with the Great Practice of the Name, *Namoamidabutsu*, 3. Being awakened to *shinjin* and Uttering the Name in gratitude, and 4. Being bestowed with Birth in the Pure Land-Enlightenment. We are able to go through this process only through the merits or virtues of Amida Buddha.

The concept of merit-transference in the Phase of Returning means that the moment we attain Enlightenment, we become One with Amida Buddha in the compassionate work of enlightening those still caught in delusion.

This concept of merit-transference is a unique feature of Jodoshinshu. It is based on the historical fact that after attaining Enlightenment, Shakyamuni Buddha returned to the world of pain and ignorance to spread the Dharma even though he realized he would be misunderstood because the nature of Enlightenment cannot be expressed in words. Clearly, the Buddha did this out of a deep concern and compassion for a suffering humanity. Shinran Shonin says:

> Those gone to the Land of Peace and Bliss
> Return to the evil world of five defilements,
> And like Shakyamuni Buddha
> Benefit sentient beings endlessly.[47]

Pure Land-Nirvana-Enlightenment is ever-active and moving towards those of us caught in the snares of evil and delusion. This activity of "benefiting-others" is a natural quality of Amida Buddha's Compassion. That is why Amida Buddha vowed that those who attain Buddhahood in his Land will return to the defiled world in order to lead those still in suffering to Enlightenment. This concept appears in the Twenty-second Vow.[48] Shinran Shonin calls this the activity of "Merit-transference in the Phase of Returning."[49] Jodoshinshu, then, is a dynamic form of Buddha-dharma which helps us to see ourselves as we truly are, and further, leads us to Enlightenment just as we are. It is a teaching in which the life-style of a householder is not altered, yet allows us to attain Enlightenment through *shinjin*.

---

47   *RTS, Jodo Wasan*, p. 48.
48   *SSZ* Vol. I, p. 10.
49   *SSZ*, Vol. II, p. 106.

Conclusion

In explaining Jodoshinshu, Shinran Shonin states that the way of *shinjin* is the "easy way to follow."[50] It is "easy" because the virtues of our Enlightenment are fulfilled by the Compassionate Amida Buddha and not by us. It is also termed "easy" because much of what Shinran Shonin presents is related to our everyday experience. If we are honest with ourselves and see our relationships with others clearly, we can see our relationship with the Other-power of Amida Buddha.

Sadly, we have doubts when something is termed "easy." We cannot readily concede our inability to strive towards the Truth in our own way. We fear that we will be "nothing" if we concede our inability, and will therefore lose our identity. As a result, we continue striving to maintain our identity, our circumstances, and our little understanding of life. That is why the "easy" way becomes the "most difficult of the difficult"[51] of ways to Enlightenment.

---

50   *RTS, Kyogyoshinsho*, p. 21.
51   *SSZ*, Vol. II. p. 44.

Yet in Shinran Shonin's view, the idea of the "most difficult of the difficult" is not negative. It is a positive statement indicating the superiority of a teaching that takes in all those who are difficult to lead to Enlightenment. In this regard, Shinran Shonin praises the way of *shinjin* as follows:

> As I contemplate the ocean-like *Great Shinjin*, I see that it does not choose between the noble and mean, priest and layman, nor does it discriminate between man and woman, old and young. The amount of evil committed is not questioned, and the length of practice is not discussed. It is neither a practice nor a good, neither abrupt nor gradual, neither meditative nor non-meditative, neither right meditation nor wrong meditation, neither contemplative nor non-contemplative, neither "while living" nor "at the end of life" neither many utterances nor one utterance. *Shinjin* is the inconceivable, indescribable, and ineffable *Serene Shinjin*. It is like the *agada* (medicine) which destroys all poisons. The medicine of Amida Buddha's Vow destroys the poisons of both our wisdom and ignorance.[52]

The phrase "most difficult of the difficult," thus means that which is difficult to attain and difficult to hear is easily attained through the Compassion of Amida Buddha. How great is the joy of those who attain the state of *shinjin*!

So in answer to the question raised at the beginning of this booklet, is Jodoshinshu still meaningful in our modern society, the answer must be an emphatic "YES!"

---

52   *RTS, Kyogyoshinsho,* pp. 113-114.

Postscript

How do we, as Jodoshinshu followers, deal with in-dividual, societal, environmental, and global problems?

The Buddha clearly stated that suffering exists because our ego-centered ignorance blinds us to the flow of Truth in our lives. That is why we are caught in the self-centered ignorance that destroys any sense of peace and harmony within us.

In this dark world of suffering, Amida Buddha calls out, urging us to reflect upon Great Compassion so that we may find joy, gratitude and meaning in our lives. And when we do, the result is a life of *Shinjin-Nembutsu*.

We are awakened to *shinjin* when we hear Amida Buddha calling out to us. We are awakened to the depths of our self-centered ignorance when we hear the Buddha's call, and at the same time, are awakened to the truth of the Buddhist life of interdependence. These are not two separate things, but two aspects of the same experience.

Our everyday life within *shinjin* is one of reflection and gratitude. Reflection makes us aware of the vastness of our inter-dependence, not only with those close to us, but also with all that exists and functions in the world. That is how we are able to live a meaningful life with all our limitations. Within that awareness, there arises a grateful sense of responsibility towards our interdependent relationships. How can we not feel an urgent need to contribute towards the well-being of all existence?

The hope of realizing a life of harmony in this world of suffering is found in reflection and gratitude. In the *Letters of Shinran (Mattosho)*, Shinran Shonin says: "The heart of those with *shinjin* are always in the Buddha Land."[53] Again he says: "Once the true and real mind is caused to arise in us, how can we remain as we were, possessed of blind passions?"[54]

We share this teaching so everyone may hear the call of Amida Buddha and participate in the flow of life that brings peace and harmony both within ourselves and within the world in which we live. We share the dynamic task expressed by Shinran's words in the *Goshosokushu:* "Let there be peace in the world. Let the Buddha-dharma spread!"[55]

---

53 Ibid., p. 662.
54 Ibid., p. 692.
55 Ibid., p. 697.

Index

This Publication has been funded by the Sustaining Membership Program of the Buddhist Churches of America, San Francisco.